Nature Up Close™
La naturaleza de cerca™

Turtles Up Close
Las tortugas

Katie Franks
Traducción al español:
Ma. Pilar Sanz

PowerKiDS
press.

& **Editorial Buenas Letras**™
New York

Published in 2008 by The Rosen Publishing Group, Inc.
29 East 21st Street, New York, NY 10010

First Edition

Editor: Jennifer Way
Book Design: Kate Laczynski
Photo Researcher: Nicole Pristash

Photo Credits: Cover, pp. 1, 5, 7, 9 (inset) 11, 13, 15, 17, 19, 21, 24 © Studio Stalio; p. 9 (main) © Shutterstock.com; p. 23 by Alessandro Bartolozzi.

Cataloging Data

Franks, Katie.
  Turtles up close–Las tortugas / Katie Franks; traducción al español: Ma. Pilar Sanz. — 1st ed.
    p. cm. — (Nature up close–La naturaleza de cerca)
  Includes index.
  ISBN 978-1-4042-7681-9 (library binding)
  1. Turtles—Juvenile literature. 2. Spanish language materials I. Title.

Manufactured in the United States of America

Websites: Due to the changing nature of Internet links, PowerKids Press and Editorial Buenas Letras have developed an online list of Web sites related to the subject of this book. This site is updated regularly. Please use this link to access the list: www.powerkidslinks.com/nuc/turtle/

Contents

Contenido

This is a turtle. Turtles are known for moving very slowly.

Esta es una tortuga. Las tortugas se conocen por sus lentos movimientos.

You can see inside a turtle's body in this picture. A few of a turtle's body parts are its head, heart, **lungs**, and **stomach**.

En esta ilustración puedes ver el cuerpo de una tortuga por dentro. Algunas partes del cuerpo son la cabeza, el corazón, los **pulmones** y el **estómago**.

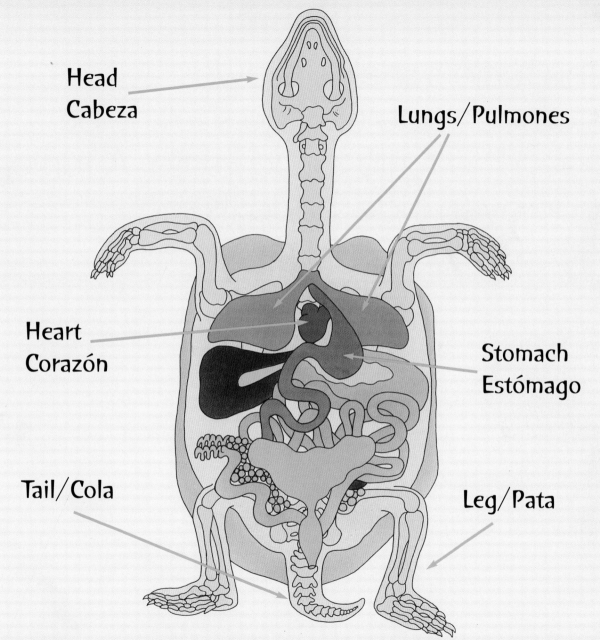

Head
Cabeza

Lungs/Pulmones

Heart
Corazón

Stomach
Estómago

Tail/Cola

Leg/Pata

7

This turtle's **shell** is shown stomach-side up. The shell helps keep the turtle's body safe. A turtle can even hide inside its shell!

Este es un **caparazón** de tortuga visto boca arriba. El caparazón protege el cuerpo de las tortugas. ¡Las tortugas se pueden esconder en su caparazón!

Some kinds of turtles live on land. Other kinds of turtles live underwater.

Algunas tortugas viven bajo el agua. Otros tipos de tortugas viven en la tierra.

Sea Turtle/Tortuga marina

Land Turtle
Tortuga terrestre

11

Turtles use their good eyesight
and strong nose to hunt
for food.

Las tortugas tienen buena vista
y narices. Las tortugas las usan
para buscar comida.

13

Some turtles hunt for fish underwater.

Algunas tortugas atrapan peces bajo el agua.

This snapping turtle is hunting a small fish. The turtle uses its wormlike **tongue** to trick the fish into swimming near its mouth.

Esta tortuga caimán mordedora está atrapando un pescado. La tortuga usa su lengua en forma de **lombriz** para atraer al pez hacia su boca.

There are animals that eat turtles. Sharks sometimes eat sea turtles.

Algunos animales comen tortugas. A veces, los tiburones comen tortugas marinas.

Female, or girl, turtles lay eggs. Baby turtles hatch, or come out, from these eggs.

Las tortugas hembra ponen huevos. Las tortugas bebé nacen de esos huevos.

Laying Eggs
Poniendo huevos

Baby Turtle
Tortuga bebé

21

People have used turtles' shells to make many things.

Los caparazones de las tortugas se usan para fabricar muchas cosas.

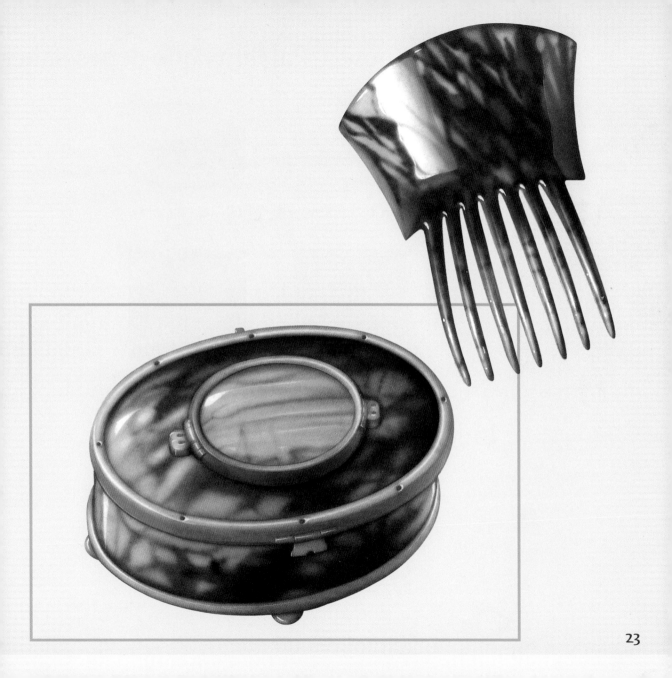

Words to Know / Palabras que debes saber

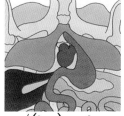

lungs/(los) pulmones

shell/(el) caparazón

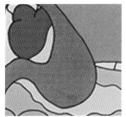

stomach/(el) estómago

tongue/(la) lengua

Index

Índice